JEAN CRAIGHEAD GEORGE

The BUFFALO *Are* BACK

PAINTINGS BY WENDELL MINOR

Dutton Children's Books · An imprint of Penguin Group (USA) Inc.

ACKNOWLEDGMENTS

The artist wishes to thank photographers Charlie Craighead and Thomas D. Mangelsen for providing valuable photo reference for the paintings in this book. Wendell's visits to tall grass prairie preserves gave him a better understanding of their vastness and beauty in order to portray them successfully. A list of sites is included on page 32. Finally, the artist wishes to give special thanks to Jean Craighead George for her friendship and continuing guidance in creating their books.

DUTTON CHILDREN'S BOOKS · A division of Penguin Young Readers Group · Published by the Penguin Group
Penguin Group (USA) Inc., 375 Hudson Street, New York, New York 10014, U.S.A. · Penguin Group (Canada), 90 Eglinton Avenue East, Suite 700, Toronto, Ontario M4P 2Y3, Canada (a division of Pearson Penguin Canada Inc.) · Penguin Books Ltd, 80 Strand, London WC2R 0RL, England · Penguin Ireland, 25 St Stephen's Green, Dublin 2, Ireland (a division of Penguin Books Ltd) · Penguin Group (Australia), 250 Camberwell Road, Camberwell, Victoria 3124, Australia (a division of Pearson Australia Group Pty Ltd) · Penguin Books India Pvt Ltd, 11 Community Centre, Panchsheel Park, New Delhi - 110 017, India · Penguin Group (NZ), 67 Apollo Drive, Rosedale, North Shore 0632, New Zealand (a division of Pearson New Zealand Ltd) · Penguin Books (South Africa) (Pty) Ltd, 24 Sturdee Avenue, Rosebank, Johannesburg 2196, South Africa
Penguin Books Ltd, Registered Offices: 80 Strand, London WC2R 0RL, England

CIP DATA AVAILABLE.

To Cyd and Carol Ann,
who praise the diversity
of the earth and the return
of the buffalo

JEAN CRAIGHEAD GEORGE

To Jean, in celebration of
her fifty years of writing
wonderful books that teach
children the wonders of nature

WENDELL MINOR

In a time long ago, an orange buffalo calf was born. He wobbled to his feet and blinked. A lark flew to the top of a six-foot blade of grass and sang as sweetly as a panpipe. A town of prairie dogs barked. The green-gold grasses of the plains rippled like waves from horizon to horizon. On that day in the mid-1800s seventy-five million buffalo roamed in North America. In little more than fifty years, there would be almost none.

What happened? The answer is a story of the American Indians, the buffalo, and the grass.

The American Indians

On the day that the calf was born the air was smoky. The Indians who lived on the plains were setting the grasses ablaze, as they had for thousands of years. The fire was good for the prairie. The calf may have been afraid of the flames, but they kept the trees from taking over the grasslands. The fire's ashes put nutrients into the soil, making the grass healthier for the buffalo that ate it.

By taking care of the grass, the Indians took care of the buffalo. In return, the buffalo took care of the Indians and the plains. Buffalo were the Indians' food and were used to make their shelter and clothing. The buffalo never ate too much grass, and their sharp hooves helped rainwater reach into the soil, keeping the prairie healthy.

The orange calf learned to roll in a dust wallow. He watched the prairie chickens show off their exotic feathers. From the Mississippi to the Rocky Mountains and from the Gulf of Mexico up into Canada, the buffalo herds grazed the Great Plains.

The Buffalo

In the mid-1800s, change came to the plains. First it was white fur hunters. They stacked the beautiful buffalo hides in pointed canoes and sold them east for profit. Then the American explorers came, who shot many animals for fun. Buffalo made good targets for the hunters because they are big and often stand still.

But it was settlers from the East and the American government that killed almost all of the buffalo herds. After the Civil War, the government bought huge tracts of land from the Indians. They forced many Indians to go to reservations and sold the land to settlers. Families from Europe and the East Coast rushed west to settle the rich black prairie land.

But there was trouble on the plains. The government broke its treaties with the Indians. So the Indians fought back and won several battles against the United States Army. Then the government saw another way to defeat the Indians. Soldiers and settlers were encouraged to shoot every buffalo they saw, or drive whole herds over cliffs. Without the buffalo for food, shelter, and clothing, the Indians could not survive on the plains.

Most of the last wild buffalo went down in dust and gunfire.

Said the great Sioux Chief Sitting Bull, who defeated General George A. Custer at the battle of Little Big Horn: "A cold wind blew across the prairie when the last buffalo fell—a death-wind for my people."

And, the settlers soon discovered, a death-wind for the prairie.

The Grass

With the death of the buffalo, the Indian Wars were over. The settlers faced a new fight—the battle of the grasses. Over the eons the prairie grasses had adapted to the Great Plains' frequent droughts by growing tough roots to hold in moisture. These roots were wide and deep and held the rich soil in place. The buffalo's sharp hooves, and the Indians' prairie fires, had helped keep the grasses healthy. But the new settlers did not understand the importance of the grass.

Early settlers were ranchers and cowboys. They brought fences and cattle to the plains. The cattle did not roam, so they ate too much of the grass within their fences. Their flat hooves packed the earth. Air and rainwater no longer reached into the soil.

Later settlers wanted to farm the land, so they tore out the grass and planted crops to sell. Steel plows and steam tractors were invented to conquer the grassland and "the great plow up" began. Wheat, corn, and soybeans were planted. These crops have shallow, fragile roots.

At first, the crops flourished in the prairie sunshine and timely rains. New railroads carried the harvests to distant markets.

Now not one orange buffalo wobbled to its feet. The larks that had once eaten the insects living in the grass did not sing. The prairie dogs were silent. Without the buffalo, without the grasses, and without the Indians to care for them, the prairie was in danger. The settlers would soon learn why.

Drought came, as it had before. Billions of grasshoppers swept down on the plains. Long ago, when drought came and grasshoppers chewed the healthy grass, the plants would grow back. Their tough roots always survived. But when the fragile crops were chewed by grasshoppers, nothing grew back.

Suddenly, the grasshoppers laid eggs and flew on. The farmers replanted their crops. They did not know they had begun to destroy the prairie.

When the buffalo lived on the prairie, their sharp hooves helped rain reach deep into the earth, and the tough roots of the grass held in the wet. Now, no moisture remained in the soil. The farmers' crops withered and died.

In the 1930s, the plowed earth finally crumbled to dust. The wind eroded the land, picking up the dust and boiling it into terrifying black clouds. The clouds rained dirt. Barns, farms, houses, and towns were buried beneath the dust. People coughed, choked, and grew ill. Many died.

Hungry and penniless, plains farmers and townsmen packed up their belongings and sold their worthless land to the government. The prairie soil had blown away. The land was no longer rich. The farmers climbed into old cars and left. The "great plow up" had been a disaster. In just over fifty years, it had destroyed the buffalo, the protective prairie grasses, and the Indians who had cared for both.

What could be done to save the prairie?

The Prairie Comeback

In the beginning of the 1900s, Americans elected a president who had once been a hunter on the Great Plains. He knew and loved the land and wanted to protect it for future generations. Nature-loving President Theodore Roosevelt especially wanted to save the buffalo. He was very fond of the great American grazer with its humped back and shaggy coat. So, he sent out scouts to look for wild buffalo.

The scouts came home with nothing—all the scouts but one. A naturalist named W. T. Hornaday looked and looked and would not give up. On a tip from a Crow Indian he rode his horse into a secluded meadow in Montana, a place that had been hidden away from the world. There before him grazed three hundred buffalo. A little orange calf wobbled to her feet and blinked. A lark flew to a blade of grass and sang as sweetly as a panpipe.

There had been seventy-five million buffalo on the plains. Now there were three hundred left in the wild. People who understood the land, led by Hornaday, knew the buffalo had to be saved. The president helped.

Roosevelt established the National Bison Range in Montana and made it illegal to shoot buffalo. Over the years, more land was set aside in western states for the great grazing herds, which were beginning to grow.

Thanks to Roosevelt, the orange calf in Montana romped with other calves and rolled in the dust. Her herd grew in numbers. Many were sent to national parks and wildlife refuges that had been established to start new herds.

As the dust storms attacked farms and cities, the government worked to save the prairie. Farmers were taught to plant and grow crops in curves, instead of straight lines. The contour plowing helped to prevent dirt from blowing away. Government workers planted trees with deep roots, to hold moisture in the soil and break the wind. When the rains returned, farmers planted grass between their curving rows of corn to hold the soil in place. Crops flourished again.

One day a young girl walked into her house in Kansas waving a six-foot blade of grass.

"Where did you find that?" her father asked. "That's buffalo grass. It's been extinct for years—or so we thought."

"In my schoolyard," she said.

"That is land that was never plowed," her father told her.

Like many older people living on the prairie, he longed to see the beautiful grasses again.

"Let's try to find more of these tall native grasses," he said. Perhaps the tall grass could come back to the plains.

People like the girl's father rounded up kids, parents, botanists, farmers, and merchants. They searched the places the plows had never reached—graveyards, old railroad beds, and crumbling fencerows. There they found small stands of the native grasses: bluestem, gamma, bunch, and buffalo grass. They raised them and sowed the seeds on abandoned farms and public lands. The grasses flourished, tall and graceful.

Groups that work to protect nature purchased thirty-thousand acres where native grasses had been grown. This nature preserve, in Kansas, is called the Tall Grass Prairie Preserve. Into the tall grass they released three hundred buffalo.

One morning not too long ago, a young man just out of graduate school galloped his horse across the Prairie Preserve, counting buffalo for the buffalo census. Suddenly he reined in his horse. An orange calf wobbled to his feet and blinked.

"Welcome, little calf," the Wichita Indian youth called. "You are America's two hundred thousand and eighty-first buffalo."

A lark flew to the top of a six-foot blade of grass and sang as sweetly as a panpipe. The buffalo are back.

Sources

Among the reference books the artist used are:

Dary, David A. *The Buffalo Book.* Athens, OH: Swallow Press, 1989.

Martin, Cy. *The Saga of the Buffalo.* New York, NY: Promontory Press, 1973.

Sample, Michael S. *Bison: Symbol of the American West.* Helena, MT: Falcon Press, 1987.

PLACES YOU CAN VISIT WHERE THE BUFFALO ROAM

National Bison Range
Moiese, Montana
http://www.fws.gov/bisonrange/nbr/

Tall Grass Prairie Preserve
Cottonwood Falls, Kansas
http://www.nps.gov/tapr

Theodore Roosevelt National Park
Medora, North Dakota
http://www.nps.gov/thro/

Willa Cather Memorial Prairie
Red Cloud, Nebraska
http://www.willacather.org/cather-prairie